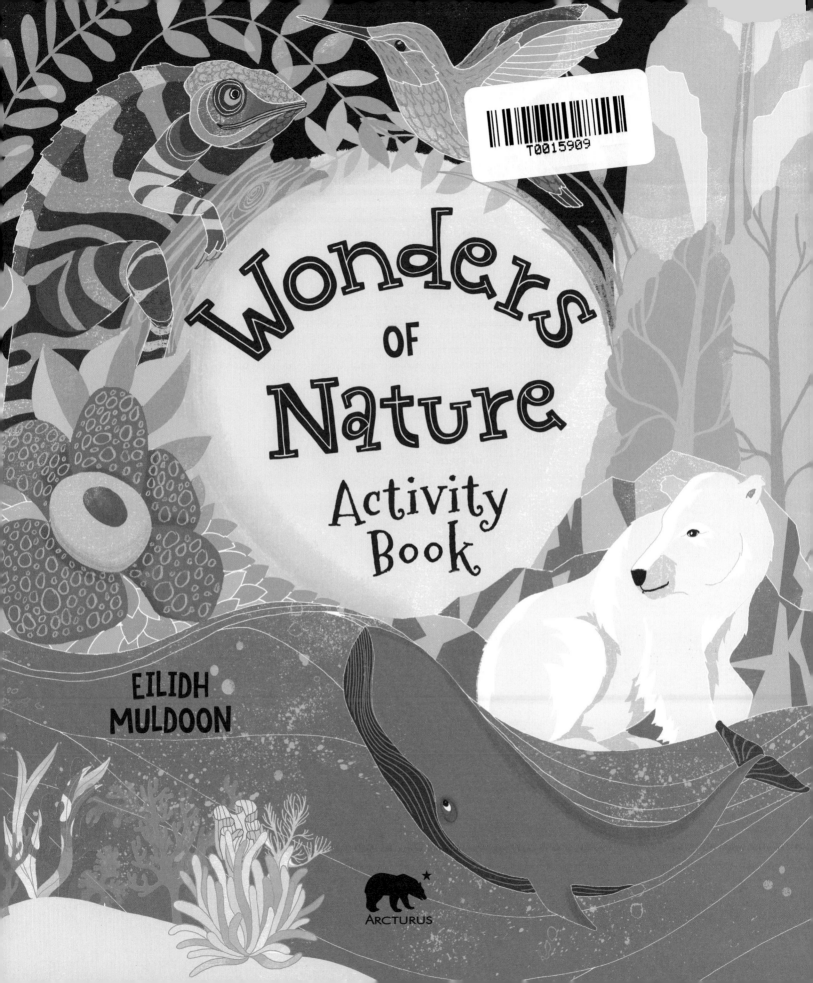

Wonders OF Nature

Activity Book

EILIDH MULDOON

ARCTURUS

ARCTURUS

This edition published in 2023 by Arcturus Publishing Limited
26/27 Bickels Yard, 151–153 Bermondsey Street,
London SE1 3HA

Author: Emily Stead
Illustrator: Eilidh Muldoon
Designer: Supriya Sahai
Editors: Becca Clunes, Lydia Halliday
Design manager: Jessica Holliland
Editorial manager: Joe Harris

ISBN: 978-1-3988-2570-3
CH010448NT
Supplier 29, Date 0423, PI 00003081

Printed in China

Wonders
OF
Nature

Are you ready to go wild and travel the planet in search of nature's most amazing natural wonders? In this stunning activity book, you'll visit hot and cold deserts, climb high mountains, and dive deep underground, meeting the wonderful wild animals and plants that live in each habitat. Complete the puzzles and activities, and learn wondrous facts along the way!

CONTENTS

GET SET, GO!

Meet the fastest animals in their class! These predators rely on their impressive speed to find food easily over land, in water, and in the air.

Cheetahs can reach a top speed of 113 kph (70 mph).

Able to accelerate from 0 to 100 kph (62 mph) in about three seconds, the cheetah is Earth's speediest land animal over short distances. Draw lines to connect the pairs, then circle the odd one out.

Swift Swimmer

Found in the Indian and Pacific Oceans, the black marlin is one of the world's fastest fish. Two of the statements below are true, and two are false. Can you guess which is which? Tick the statements that you think are true.

The black marlin spears fish with its long nose. ☐

Black marlins prefer to live in temperate waters. ☐

All black marlins are born female. ☐

Black marlins don't live as long as swordfish. ☐

Horsing Around

Scientists have recorded the common horsefly reaching speeds of 145 kph (90 mph). Which shadow matches this speedy insect exactly?

There are more than 1,300 species of horsefly.

TALL TREES

The tallest trees in the world stand sky high in California's national parks, USA.

Towering redwoods can easily reach heights of over 90 m (295 ft), while giving us oxygen, storing carbon, and providing a home to wildlife from insects to birds to mammals.

Add up the numbers on these tree trunks to find the oldest redwood among them.

Giant redwoods can live for more than 3,000 years. Incredible!

A

7

101

500

346

1,435

B

11

99

425

380

1,234

C

18

75

423

621

1,501

8

Genuine Giants

Meet five more enormous trees that all loom large at over 95 m (310 ft).

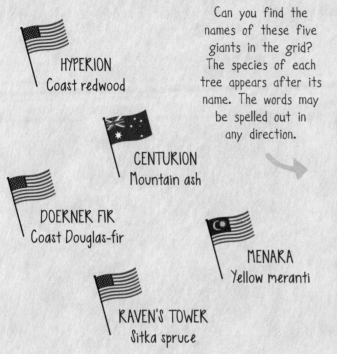

HYPERION
Coast redwood

CENTURION
Mountain ash

DOERNER FIR
Coast Douglas-fir

MENARA
Yellow meranti

RAVEN'S TOWER
Sitka spruce

Can you find the names of these five giants in the grid? The species of each tree appears after its name. The words may be spelled out in any direction.

D	V	G	Y	M	J	V	N	I	Z	R	O
F	Q	T	R	U	C	O	I	S	D	U	L
M	J	B	A	L	I	P	O	K	B	S	I
I	C	D	V	R	T	Y	R	G	F	P	R
B	K	V	E	F	B	Q	U	D	C	R	C
Z	L	P	N	G	R	H	T	X	M	U	H
S	Y	C	S	Z	M	I	N	U	E	C	D
H	I	Q	T	R	F	K	E	J	N	E	P
G	F	Y	O	D	X	T	C	S	A	E	I
V	Z	B	W	C	M	Y	Q	B	R	S	N
K	Y	D	E	J	V	K	G	F	A	I	P
D	O	E	R	N	E	R	F	I	R	H	I

Tropical Titan

The tallest tropical tree is a yellow meranti. It was discovered on the island of Borneo in 2016 and given the name Menara.

Circle these three close-ups in Menara's canopy.

Menara measures a massive 100.8 m (330.7 ft) tall.

CURIOUS FOSSILS

Fossils are the remains of animals or plants that have been preserved over a very long time. Many fossils are discovered in rock, but they can also be found in ice, mud, or even amber. Fossils give us a snapshot of creatures that lived millions of years ago.

Start in the middle, counting from the letter F, and circle every third letter in the fossil to reveal the name of an ancient sea creature. Clue: the first letter would be A.

AMAZING AMBER

Plants and animals can become trapped in the sticky substance that is released from the bark of pine and fir trees. As the sap hardens into amber, organisms can remain perfectly preserved for millions of years.

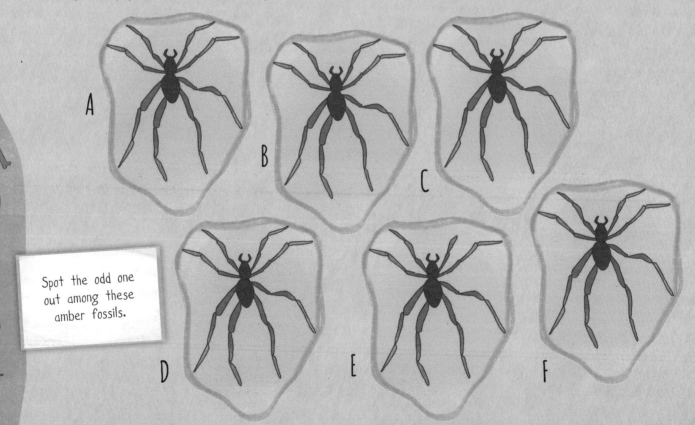

Spot the odd one out among these amber fossils.

Famous Fossils

Among the most fascinating fossils are those of bones belonging to dinosaurs. Dinosaur fossils have been found in every continent, and they give us a glimpse of the lives of many incredible species.

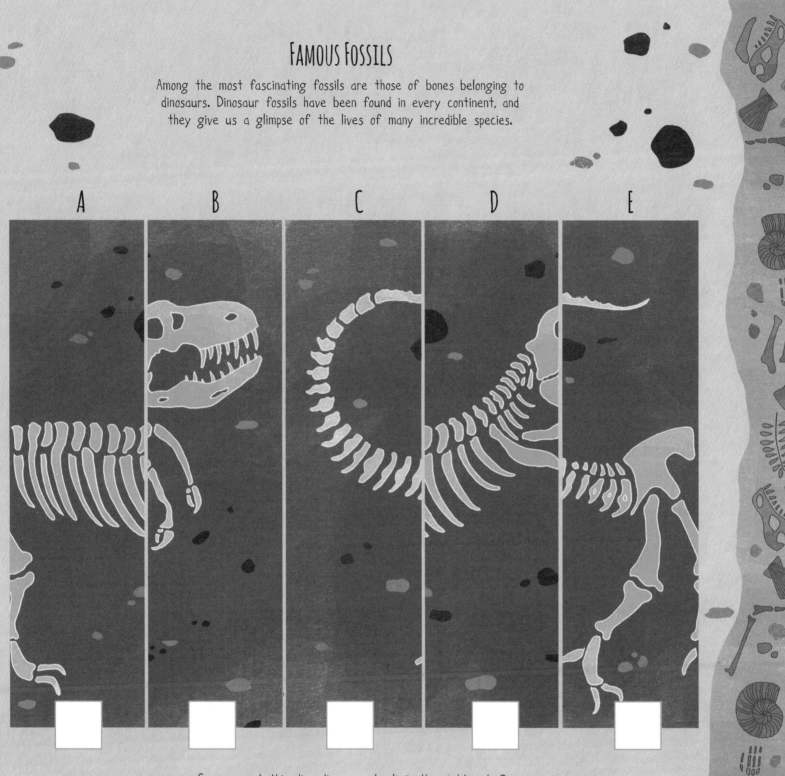

Can you put this dino discovery back in the right order?

IN BLOOM

Flowers are usually the most beautiful part of a plant, also called the blooms, or blossoms. While you may be familiar with fragrant roses or tulips, did you know that there is a flower called the "corpse flower", or that some blooms appear more like animals than plants? Read on to meet three fascinating flowers.

Crack the number code to discover the name of this heavenly bloom.

A	B	C	D	E	F	G	H	I	J	K	L	M
26		24										

N	O	P	Q	R	S	T	U	V	W	X	Y	Z
		11		9				5			2	

25 18 9 23   12 21   11 26 9 26 23 18 8 22

....

TITAN ARUM

The corpse flower (*titan arum*) is one of the smelliest plants on Earth, with an awful aroma of rotting flesh. Luckily, it flowers just once every seven to nine years, with the bloom only lasting a day or so.

The tallest ever corpse flower measured 3.10 m tall (10 ft 2 in.)

28
42
35
56
14
21
49

Study the numbers, and figure out which times table is represented.

MONKEYING AROUND

The monkey face orchid is a very rare species that only grows at high altitudes. It's not hard to guess how this flower got its name, since it has two "eyes" and a monkey-shaped nose and mouth.

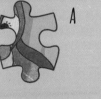

Which two pieces complete the jigsaw puzzle of this fascinating flower?

A

B

C

D

ANIMALS IN DANGER

Hundreds of species of animals are endangered, or at risk of becoming extinct. Humans pose the biggest threat to animals, through the destruction of the creatures' habitats, hunting, pollution, and climate change.

Which of these rhinos has left the most footprints, the adult or the baby?

Answer:

There are thought to be fewer than 80 Sumatran rhinos left in the world.

MANGO MIX-UP

This red-haired primate is native to the tropical rain forests of Southeast Asia. Rearrange the letters on the mangos to spell the name of this endangered ape, which means "human of the forest."

A R G O N A U T N

FEELING BLUE

Blue whales live in all the world's oceans except the Arctic, and they are close to extinction following centuries of being hunted.

How many beautiful blue whales can you count above?

THE GREAT BARRIER REEF

The glorious Great Barrier Reef is the world's largest coral reef, where corals have grown for as long as 25 million years. While climate change and pollution threaten the health of the reef, scientists are working hard to preserve this natural wonder.

Rearrange these tiles to make a coral reef scene.

Pretty Parrotfish

Tropical parrotfish shimmer in rainbow shades, often swimming in schools of several hundred fish.

Circle ONLY the fish showing numbers that are multiples of 5.

Underwater Treasures

Hundreds of species of fish, animals, algae, and corals all inhabit this remarkable reef system. Complete the puzzle so that each picture appears once in every row, column, and mini grid.

BRILLIANT BEETLES

From arid deserts to the polar ice caps, scientists have discovered about 400,000 species of beetles worldwide. These winged bugs have six legs and a hard shell, and they come in all kinds of shades and patterns. Some are predators, while others are useful pollinators.

101

Dung beetles feast on the nutrients in the poop that larger animals leave behind. Find the calculation that matches this total on one of the dung balls below.

A
$24 \times 5 = $ ☐

B
$9 \times 11 = $ ☐

C
$127 - 26 = $ ☐

D
$51 \times 2 = $ ☐

One dung beetle can roll more than 1,100 times its weight—the equivalent of a human pulling six large buses!

HORNED HERBIVORES

The male rhinoceros beetle uses its antler-like horns to battle fellow beetles when searching for tasty tree sap.

Circle the beetle that you think is the female among the colony.

MUSICAL BUG

Insects are among the world's weirdest creatures—some are so strange that they seem make-believe! Use the grid to help you find out the name of the musical instrument that gives this beetle its name.

	a	b	c	d
1	B	G	I	D
2	M	V	U	P
3	I	T	F	O
4	N	E	L	R

b2 c1 d3 c4 n3 a4

....

19

CHANGING SEASONS

The cherry tree changes its appearance with each season that passes.
Take a look at its amazing transformation throughout the year.

BEAUTIFUL BLOSSOMS

Spring days see the cherry tree produce spectacular pink blossoms, since the tree blooms for about two to three weeks.

Find the blossom that matches this picture on the cherry tree.

Picnicking beneath cherry blossom trees is a Japanese tradition because the bloom is the country's national flower.

Do you think there are more than 40 cherries on this tree? Make an estimate, then count to check.

While every cherry tree produces fruit, not all cherries are edible to humans. Smaller cherries make a tasty summer snack for birds.

START

Falling Leaves

As the seasons change again, bringing cooler days, the cherry tree begins to shed its leaves. Join this falling leaf on its journey to the ground.

Trees that shed their leaves each year are called deciduous trees, while the leaves of evergreen trees remain green in every season.

FINISH

Branching Out

As wintry weather arrives, the leaves have all disappeared, leaving bare branches. The tree conserves its energy, ready for the cycle to begin again in spring.

Choose a branch, then draw a friend for this robin.

DESERT CONDITIONS

About one-quarter of the land surface of our planet is
so dry that it is classed as desert. Plants and animals that
live there have learned to adapt to desert conditions,
where little rain falls and temperatures are extreme.

Circle only the numbers
that are multiples of 4
on the desert plain.

8

3

40

42   38

4

11

2

44

32

16   10   50

7   12

14

28

21   24

25

Desert Storm

Dangerous desert dust storms with winds that blow at speeds of up to 100 Kph (60 mph) whip up sand and dust.

Can you spot five meerkats taking shelter from the storm in the Kalahari Desert?

A   B   C   D   E

Too Cold to Snow

Very little rain or snow falls in freezing Antarctica. In fact, it's so dry that scientists consider it to be a desert. Winter temperatures there can drop as low as −89.2 °C (−128.6 °F).

Rearrange this snowy scene in the right order.

DESERT DWELLERS

Camels are perfectly designed for the hot, dry conditions of desert life, and they can make their water supplies last for long periods—sometimes months.

Follow the lines to find out which camel in the caravan will reach the watering hole.

A · B · C · D

Super Survivors

Scorpions are ancient animals that existed long before dinosaurs came along. The venom in a scorpion's tail is used both to catch prey, and to protext itself. Pick out the shadow that is an exact match for this prehistoric predator.

A

B

C

D

Saharan Snakes

Add up the numbers on these three snakes that reside in the Sahara Desert to find the deadliest among the trio. The snake with the highest total is the most venomous.

DESERT HORNED VIPER

=

9

27

4

24

7   12

=

NUBIAN SPITTING COBRA

EGYPTIAN COBRA

2   35

11

=

COOL CRYSTALS

From valuable diamonds to beautiful shapes formed in ice or salt, crystals are naturally formed when liquids cool, in a process called crystallization. The Cave of the Crystals was discovered in Chihuahua, Mexico, in 2000 CE. It contains breathtaking crystals that measure 11 m (36 ft) in length.

Find the three pieces that complete the jigsaw puzzle.

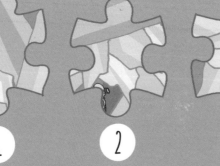

1   2   3   4

Striking Snowflakes

Snowflakes are made up of tiny ice crystals, created when water freezes in the air. As many as 200 crystals fuse together to make each snowflake.

Complete the other halves of these charming crystals.

Unearthing Geodes

Geodes are hollow rocks that contain crystals inside. They can range in size from tiny—less than 1 cm (0.4 in)—to 11 m (36 ft) long, and they are often found in desert or volcanic environments.

Find the odd one out among this geode collection.

A

D

C

B

E

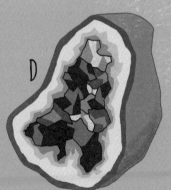

JAW-DROPPING JUMPERS

When it comes to champion jumpers, the animal kingdom puts Olympic athletes to shame jumping—farther, higher, and faster than humans! Some species jump as a means of moving, while others leap out of reach of predators.

Connect the spider pairs, then circle the odd one out.

The jumping spider can jump 100 times its own body length (similar to a human jumping the length of two jumbo jets!)

LEGENDARY LEAPERS

Mostly found in tropical regions and rain forests, tree frogs can jump to about 2.1 m (7 ft)— that's 50 times the length of their own body!

Follow the paths to discover where this little frog will land.

JUMP ON BOARD!

Fleas are parasites—animals that live and feed on other creatures. While these tiny insects can't crawl or fly, they are unbeatable jumpers.

A

B

C

Which close-up picture does not belong to the flea?

ALL ABOUT ALGAE

Algae are important organisms that produce up to 80 percent of our planet's oxygen. Scientists estimate that there are about 27,000 species of algae on Earth, from tiny microalgae to giant kelp. Though some species look like plants, algae do not have true roots, stems, or leaves.

Algae form the base of the marine food chain— without these organisms, there would be no fish or other sea creatures.

Find a path through this maze of aquatic algae.   START

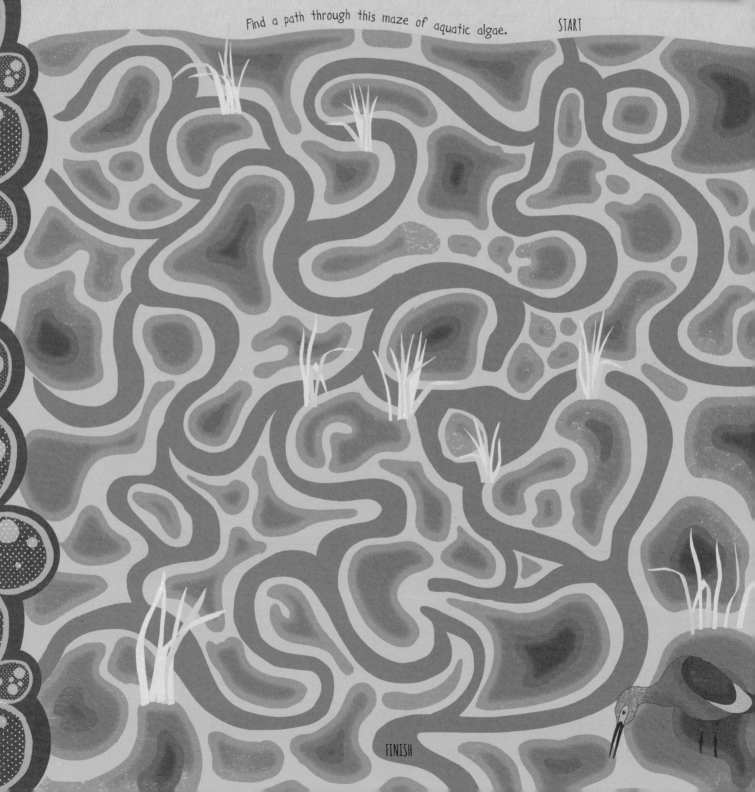

FINISH

Incredible Algae

Algae can be used to make all kinds of useful and eco-friendly products.

R	T	G	H	L	B	Y	D	W	J	I	F	Q	C
X	S	U	A	N	I	M	A	L	F	E	E	D	I
S	U	R	F	B	O	A	R	D	S	B	R	H	T
H	D	C	V	S	F	W	Y	K	U	X	T	L	S
B	O	B	X	Q	U	J	O	S	L	H	I	J	A
L	J	I	F	M	E	V	C	F	K	W	L	V	L
G	K	H	L	O	L	E	Y	B	S	M	I	G	P
V	F	M	W	K	O	H	J	E	C	O	Z	K	O
Y	Q	P	S	M	E	D	I	C	I	N	E	S	I
S	E	O	H	S	G	N	I	N	N	U	R	L	B

Find eight things made from amazing algae in the grid— some may surprise you! The words may be spelled out in any direction.

BIOFUEL	SURFBOARDS
FOOD	FERTILIZER
RUNNING SHOES	MEDICINES
ANIMAL FEED	BIOPLASTIC

Giant Grower

Kelp is the largest species of marine algae, and can grow up to a gigantic 53 m (175 ft). It provides a habitat for many sea species.

Find five fish nibbling the Kelp.

WINGS OF WONDER

With wing sizes varying from teeny to titanic, many birds flap their feathered forelimbs to fly. Hummingbird species move their wings at different speeds that are too fast for the human eye to follow. Some species can flutter their wings up to 80 times per second.

Which path will lead this hummingbird to some delicious nectar?

Acrobatic hummingbirds can fly backward and even upside down!

WANDERING WONDER

At 3.65 m (12 ft), the largest wingspan in the world belongs to this bird. But do you know its name?

Complete the key, then use the reverse alphabet code to find out.

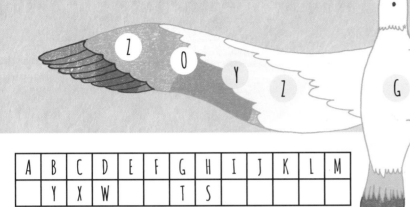

A	B	C	D	E	F	G	H	I	J	K	L	M
Y	X	W				T	S					

N	O	P	Q	R	S	T	U	V	W	X	Y	Z
		K	J				F			C	B	A

....

FLIGHTLESS FUNCTIONS

Large and heavy, the ostrich is one of a few rare bird species that cannot fly. Its short wings, however, prove useful in a number of other ways.

Which of the following does it NOT use its wings for?

☐ Mating displays

☐ Fans to keep cool

☐ To balance when running

☐ For defending themselves

☐ Camouflage

THE WATER CYCLE

The water cycle is the journey that water takes as it moves between the air and Earth's surface. The five important steps in this recycling process are evaporation, condensation, precipitation, percolation, and collection.

Unscramble the letters below to find the names of the steps of the water cycle.

As air cools, droplets are formed.

CANONISEDNOT

_____

Water falls to the ground in the form of rain, hail, sleet, or snow.

RECITATIONPIP

_____

Water is heated by the Sun and turns into gas.

OVARIANPOET

_____

Water slowly soaks into the ground over time.

PELICANROOT

_____

Rainwater runs over land and collects in lakes, rivers, and oceans.

COLICLENTO

_____

Shifting States

Water can be found on Earth in three states of matter—solid, liquid, and gas.

Study the pictures, then draw lines from each picture to the correct state.

GAS

LIQUID

SOLID

In Earth's atmosphere

In oceans, rivers, lakes, and streams—even underground

In glaciers, icebergs, and snow

Fast Floods

Too much rainwater can make sea and river levels rise quickly, flooding nearby areas and causing damage.

Study these flooded scenes— can you spot six differences in the second picture?

FACT OR FAIRY TALE?

In the icy waters of the Arctic, narwhals really do exist!
These long-tusked creatures, known as the "unicorns of
the sea," are in fact a species of whale.

Circle all the numbers that
appear in the five times table,
then cross out the ones that
appear in the four times table.
There should be an odd one
left out.

A narwhal's tusk—
most commonly found on
males—is actually an
oversized tooth. Some
narwhals may have two
tusks, while others have
none at all.

10

4

12

15

24

30

36

41

45

50

SQUID OF LEGENDS

The kraken is a legendary sea monster of colossal size, said to have appeared off the coasts of Norway. Did it exist, or was it dreamed up by superstitious sailors? Bring this kraken to life using pens or crayons.

AMAZING AMPHIBIAN

The baby-faced axolotl lives in the freshwater rivers and lakes of Mexico City. This endangered species has the amazing ability to regrow body parts. Follow the lines to find a snack for this hungry axolotl.

TROPICAL STORMS

Tropical storms begin life over Earth's oceans, close to the equator. Warm, moist air rises and sucks in more air to form a swirling cloud that produces heavy rainfall and powerful winds. In North America, these storms become hurricanes when winds reach speeds of more than 119 kph (74 mph.)

Circle the three close-ups in the big picture.

Hurricanes are named by the World Meteorological Organization, with each storm named in alphabetical order, such as Hurricane Andrew, then Hurricane Benjamin.

SWIRLING STORM

A circular storm that forms over the southern Pacific and Indian Oceans is known as a cyclone. A cyclone brings heavy rains and strong winds as it hits land.

A

B

C

D

E

F

Arrange the pieces of this shot from space back into the right order.

BREAKING WAVES

Tsunamis are giant ocean waves that grow in size and power as they reach the shore. A tsunami can be caused by an underwater earthquake or a volcanic explosion. Use pens or pencils to decorate this huge wave.

The word "hurricane" comes from the word "Huracan," a Mayan god.

NATURAL TREASURES

In every corner of the world, there are natural treasures to be found—extraordinary objects made by animals, plants, and our planet itself. Most jewels are mined from the Earth, but pearls come from an animal called an oyster.

Which path will lead the diver to discover a special treasure?

SAFFRON SUDOKU

Saffron is the world's most expensive spice, and it was once traded at the same price as gold. From each hand-picked crocus flower, just three stigmas (the sticky part in the middle of a flower) are collected and used in cooking.

Complete the puzzle so that each crocus flower appears once in every row, column, and mini grid.

LUXURY FABRIC

Cashmere is a supersoft wool obtained from goats that live in the Kashmir region. Four goat fleeces are needed to produce a single cashmere sweater, resulting in an expensive price tag for this item.

Circle the goat that is not like the others.

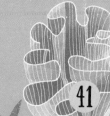

PRECIOUS METALS

Metals are minerals that are found underground in rocks, which are then separated using heat. A metal is described as "precious" when its value is worth more than most other metals. Precious metals have many uses beyond their natural beauty.

Dig for ten of Earth's most precious metals in the grid below! The words may be spelled out in any direction.

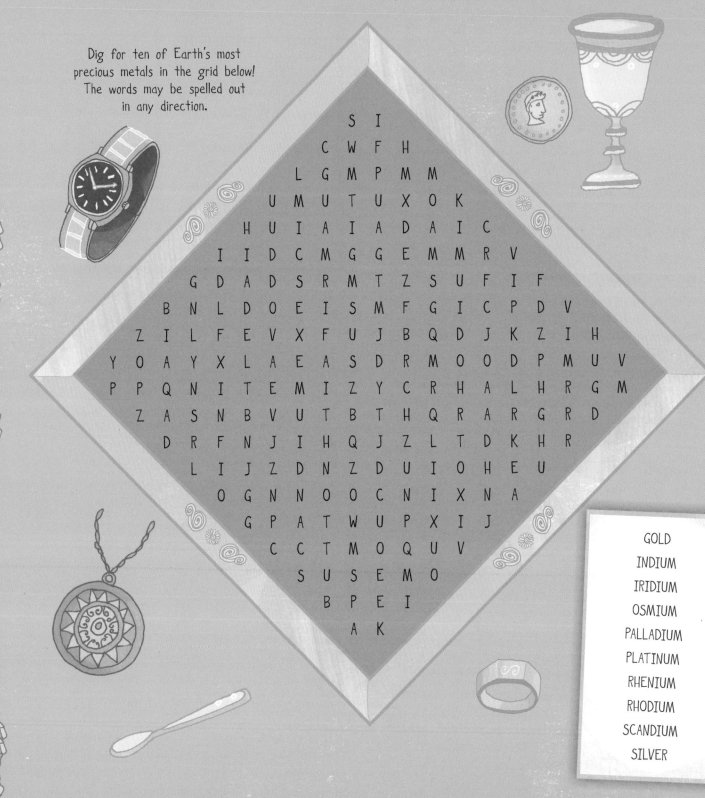

```
              S I
            C W F H
          L G M P M M
        U M U T U X O K
      H U I A I A D A I C
    I I D C M G G E M M R V
  G D A D S R M T Z S U F I F
B N L D O E I S M F G I C P D V
Z I L F E V X F U J B Q D J K Z I H
Y O A Y X L A E A S D R M O O D P M U V
P P Q N I T E M I Z Y C R H A L H R G M
Z A S N B V U T B T H Q R A R G R D
D R F N J I H Q J Z L T D K H R
  L I J Z D N Z D U I O H E U
    O G N N O O C N I X N A
      G P A T W U P X I J
        C C T M O Q U V
          S U S E M O
            B P E I
              A K
```

GOLD
INDIUM
IRIDIUM
OSMIUM
PALLADIUM
PLATINUM
RHENIUM
RHODIUM
SCANDIUM
SILVER

GOLD RUSH

Found in rocks, gold has been desirable to humans since ancient times. This soft and beautiful metal can be melted and cast into blocks called ingots.

The number on each ingot is the sum of the numbers on the two touching ingots below it. Fill in the missing numbers.

432   951

233

50   535

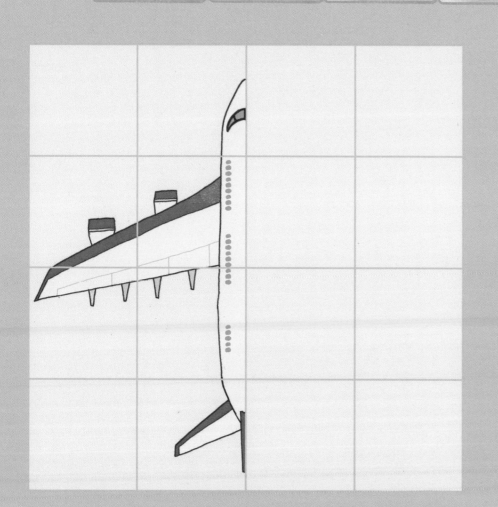

CHANGING VALUES

Aluminum (sometimes spelled aluminium) once cost more than gold before prices plummeted after it became cheaper to produce. Now the metal is commonly used in everything from vehicles to household goods.

Aluminum is the most abundant metal in the Earth's crust.

Aluminum is used to build planes because it is strong and lightweight. Draw the other half of this aircraft in the grid.

ALL ABOUT CLOUDS

Look up in the sky, and you'll never see two clouds that are the same.
These floating collections of water droplets can be found in the sky from about
2,000 m (6,600 ft) from the ground to more than 6,000 m (20,000 ft).

START

Help this griffon vulture make its way through the cloud maze.

This high-flying bird can reach heights of almost 300 m (more than 11,500 ft) in the air.

FINISH

Changing Clouds

Meteorologists (people who study weather) classify clouds according to their shape and where they are found in the sky. Add the different cloud types to the grid, so that only one of each type appears in every row, column, and mini grid.

Stratus

Nimbus

Cumulus

Cirrus

Cirrostratus

Cirrocumulus

Precipitation Puzzle

Precipitation falls from clouds in different forms and can be liquid or solid. Rain, snow, sleet, and hail are among the most common types of precipitation.

Can you connect each picture to its description?

B

Falling ice crystals

Sleet

Falling balls of ice

A

Rain

C

D

Rain that freezes as it falls

Falling drops of liquid water

Hail

Snow

PRICKLY PLANTS

Cacti are perfectly adapted to surviving in the hot and dry deserts of South and North America. These spiky plants can store large amounts of water in their stems and roots, and they can grow from tiny to a super-tall 20 m (66 ft) high.

Cross out every other letter on this cactus to learn the name of a plant that's an expert at storing water.

S T U B C I C O U V L P E R N I T

Some species of cacti can live for up to 300 years.

Spiky Saguaro

Starting at number 1, join the dots to reveal the tallest cactus in the United States.

The world's tallest ever saguaro cactus measured 23.8 m (78 ft).

Ant Allies

Helpful ants protect cacti from bacteria and fungi by regularly cleaning the plant, while they enjoy its sugary nectar.

Find six ants hidden on this prickly pear cactus.

WONDERFUL BUTTERFLIES

Beautiful butterflies can be found on every continent except Antarctica, where temperatures are too cold for these amazing insects to fly. A butterfly goes through a fascinating transformation, called a metamorphosis, during the course of its life.

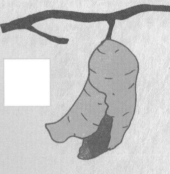

Starting with the egg, order these pictures from 1–6 to show the life cycle of a butterfly.

A group of monarch butterflies is called a "flutter."

Natural Beauty

With their striking shades and fluttering wings, butterflies are among the most fascinating of all insect species. Use your pens or pencils to copy and shade in the patterns on the butterfly's wing, or create your own.

Butterflies of Europe

Europe is home to almost 500 species of butterfly, from the shimmering common blue to the endangered violet copper. Complete the puzzle to show one of each butterfly species in each column, grid, and mini grid.

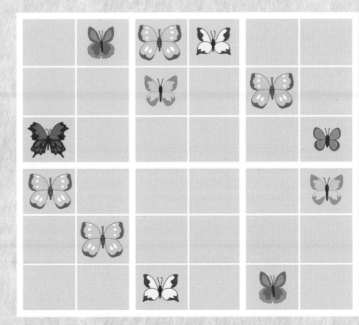

RUGGED ROCKS

Considered to be one of the seven wonders of the natural world, the vast Grand Canyon is found in Arizona, USA. The giant gorge as we know it today may have started out as a series of smaller canyons about 70 million years ago.

Write down the squares where you spot each of the following:

....

....

....

SACRED SITE

Uluru in central Australia is an enormous, ancient rock that is sacred to the indigenous people who have lived in the territory for tens of thousands of years.

Which pieces complete the picture?

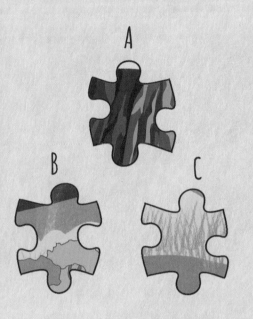

A

B   C

GIANT'S CAUSEWAY

This famous natural landmark in Northern Ireland, UK, is made up of about 40,000 hexagonal stepping stones. It was formed 60 million years ago following a volcanic eruption.

Find a path from start to finish, doubling your number each time.

FINISH

60 124 180 360 2008 4088
32 64 246 1004 2046 8084
     48 128 1023 4096 16384
         256 512 2048 8192
                1024 4092
16
    4   24   1006   16368
                              4088
8   12   56   8183   32736
START   112
    2   48   10
                          65472

51

ARCTIC ADAPTATIONS

The freezing, windy climate of the Arctic demands the wildlife that lives there to be well adapted for survival, whether land animals or sea dwellers. A thick layer of blubber keeps the orca whale warm, while its black back camouflages it from the creatures it preys on above the surface of the ocean, and its white belly disguises it from the creatures below.

Known as killer whales, orcas are also the largest member of the dolphin family.

Can you find six differences between the two images?

Polar Pal

This animal's adaptations include white fur to act as camouflage, thick layers of fat for insulation, and a strong stomach to digest a high-fat diet that gives maximum energy.

Connect the dots to reveal the snowy survivor.

Frequent Flyer

Arctic terns hold the record for the longest migration in the animal kingdom—they fly from the Arctic Circle to the Antarctic Circle every year.

How many of these special seabirds can you count?

SURPRISING CARNIVORES

While many plants are a source of food for insects and animals, some plants turn the tables and feed on insects and small prey such as frogs and rodents instead. These cunning carnivores have developed tricky adaptations, from sweet-smelling nectar to snapping jaw-like leaves and sticky traps.

Brighten up this pitcher plant in vibrant reds and greens.

The pitcher plant has pitfall traps that capture prey in its slippery nectar.

TRAPPED!

The carnivorous Venus flytrap captures insects in its sticky, snapping leaves. The insects are then digested during the days that follow. Trace the paths to reveal which trap will get a tasty treat.

BOGUS BUG-EATER

Thirsty insects are attracted to the "raindrops" on the end of the cape sundew's leafy tentacles. But these "drops" aren't water—instead, a sticky substance traps prey.

Circle any numbers that are not multiples of 3, then write the remaining numbers in the boxes. The three-digit number will tell you how many sundew species grow.

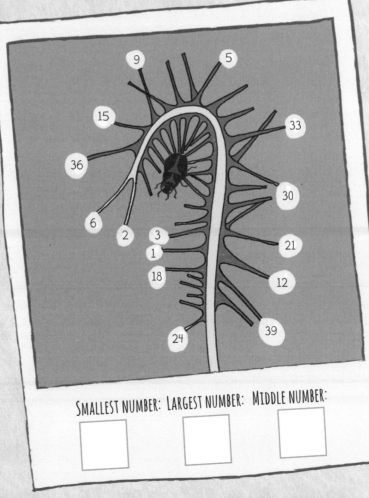

9 5
15 33
36 30
6
2 3
1 21
18 12
24 39

SMALLEST NUMBER: LARGEST NUMBER: MIDDLE NUMBER:

AMAZING BEES

Bees are expert pollinators of crops eaten by humans and animals, including fruit, vegetables, and nuts. Their important work means that many plants and food crops can reproduce. Meanwhile, humans have eaten the sweet honey produced by honeybees since ancient times.

Make your way through the honeycomb maze in the order of the alphabet.

START

FINISH

Ingenious Insects

Busy bees can make more than just honey! Can you find these five useful products produced by bees in the grid?

HONEY—a sweetener that soothes burns, and treat coughs

BEESWAX—used to make candles, furniture polish, and cosmetics

PROPOLIS—used to heal wounds and treat infections since ancient times

ROYAL JELLY—eaten for health and well-being

BEE VENOM—used as a medicine to treat pain

The word search grid (hexagonal letters):

M P C R B R L X B H J
S I H E E O J A I L S
P F G L E Y G W K T Y
X R X S V A X S P V I
K W O O E L L E B X H
H O X P N J Z B L W
O R O M E L I N
R E L L N
Y

Cutting Edge

Female leaf-cutting bees use their jaws as scissors to cut sections from leaves. These leafy extractions are then used to build bees' nests.

Which branch is a mirror image of the one on the left?

A   B   C

NATURE'S RAINBOW

The natural world is home to creatures that dazzle in all shades of the rainbow, either to impress a mate, keep predators away, or blend in with their habitats. The chameleon is one creature that can change shades for all three of these reasons, as well as to control its body temperature.

Find the three missing pieces to complete the jigsaw puzzle.

A   B   C   D

Pretty Deadly

The vibrant mandarin fish looks beautiful, but smells terrible! It releases both poison and a foul stench to warn off predators. Complete the picture using the shaded dots to help you.

The mandarin fish does not have scales—a stinky mucus covers its body instead.

In the Pink

Pretty flamingos get their pastel shade from their diet—pigments in the algae and shrimp they eat turn their feathers pink.

Spot six differences between these flamboyances of flamingos.

EXPLOSIVE VOLCANOES

A volcano is one of Earth's most dangerous natural features. When one erupts, molten rock (called magma), ash, and gas are expelled from inside the volcano through holes in the Earth's surface. When the Indonesian volcano Krakatoa erupted in 1883, it was one of the deadliest eruptions in modern history. Hundreds of nearby villages were destroyed.

Follow the lava flow from Krakatoa's crater to the finish.

START

Red-hot lava can reach temperatures of 1,200°C (2,190°F).

FINISH

R I N B
U M
S E A

Deep-Sea Danger

Scientists estimate that there are more than one million volcanoes located underwater, many of which are extinct.

Unscramble the letters to learn another name for these undersea volcanoes. Hint: this is also the name for an underwater boat.

S _ _ _ _ _ _ _ _

Eruption Disruption

Eyjafjallajökull is an active volcano in Iceland. When it erupted in 2010, it sent a huge ash cloud into the air that halted more than 100,000 flights across Europe.

Estimate how many letters make up the name of Iceland's famous volcano, then see if you were right.

ESTIMATE: [ ]

COUNT: [ ]

EYJAFJALLAJÖKULL

GLISTENING GEMSTONES

Earth's natural treasures, gems, are dug out of rocks in the form of crystals. The more valuable crystals are then cut and polished into gemstones that come in many shapes, sizes, and shimmering shades. The Crown Jewels of the United Kingdom are a collection of royal jewels kept under lock and key at the Tower of London.

Spot six differences between these priceless pictures.

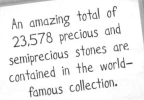

An amazing total of 23,578 precious and semiprecious stones are contained in the world-famous collection.

Ancient Treasures

Gemstones have fascinated humans for centuries. The Romans believed that a diamond was a piece of a falling star, while the ancient Greeks thought that the same gem was a teardrop from the gods. For each collection of gemstones, draw the next one in the sequence.

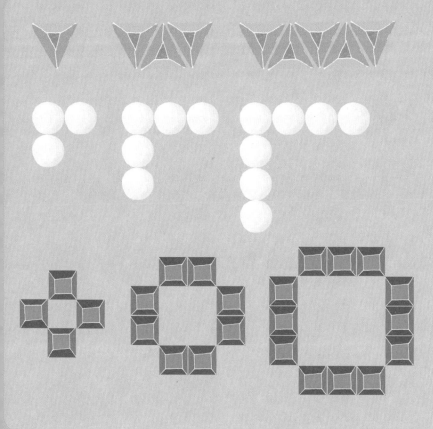

Hidden Gems

Diamond, emerald, ruby, and sapphire are the only four stones described as "precious", while hundreds more "semiprecious" gems exist.

How many beautiful gems and minerals can you unearth in the grid? The words may be spelled out in any direction.

AMBER	OBSIDIAN
AMETHYST	PEARL
DIAMOND	QUARTZ
EMERALD	RUBY
GARNET	SAPPHIRE

A	F	C	M	L	J	U	I	P	E	Q	L
Z	G	V	W	P	O	N	X	M	V	U	D
U	D	E	F	C	T	O	S	P	H	A	P
S	N	M	B	E	S	B	K	M	F	R	E
A	M	E	T	H	Y	S	T	P	W	T	A
P	S	R	M	U	N	I	W	M	E	Z	R
P	K	A	C	V	O	D	B	N	I	C	L
H	T	L	U	R	V	I	R	M	K	M	N
I	J	D	E	Z	S	A	F	P	T	D	S
R	V	B	O	D	G	N	C	M	B	W	A
E	M	I	P	T	L	X	F	P	E	Y	K
A	G	D	N	O	M	A	I	M	I	L	H

INCREDIBLE JOURNEYS

Some creatures make impressive migrations, crossing oceans into different continents to find a temporary home. Most travel in search of food or a place to breed and raise their families, while some try to escape extreme temperatures. On remote Christmas Island, millions of crabs migrate across the land to lay their eggs in the ocean.

The roads of Christmas Island become rivers of red each year, with crabs en route from rain forest to ocean.

How many crabs can you see?

Turtle Tourists

Most sea turtles migrate to find food or somewhere to nest in warmer areas as the seasons change. Often these journeys can be thousands of miles long.

L__TH_RB_CK

Add the missing letters to complete the names in this trio of wandering turtles.

L_GG_RH__D

GR___N

Migrant Monarch

The monarch butterfly is famous for its mega migration from the northern US states and southern Canada to California and Mexico. Guided by their internal magnetic compass and the Sun, monarchs enjoy warmer temperatures much farther south.

Follow the butterfly's path on the map from the USA to Mexico.

START   USA

MEXICO   FINISH

65

START

FINISH

Follow the path
of a tiny particle as
it lights up the sky.

THE NORTHERN LIGHTS

The Aurora Borealis, or Northern Lights, is a natural light show that can be
seen in the skies around the north pole, from as far away as Alaska to Norway.
The aurora takes place when tiny magnetized particles from the Sun burn up in
Earth's atmosphere, producing shimmering shades and flashes of light.

Norse Myths

The Northern Lights have fascinated many cultures for millennia. The Vikings believed that the aurora was light reflected from the shields of the Valkyries—mighty female warriors.

Copy the warrior's portrait into the empty grid.

Alaskan Sight

Visit the Northern Lights, and you may well meet an Alaskan moose. One of these silhouettes is different from the others.

Can you spot the odd one out?

DEADLY PREDATORS

Some of the deadliest predators on the planet can be found underwater—in our oceans, as well as in freshwater rivers and lakes. Often mistaken for a stone or coral, the venomous stonefish is an expert in camouflage. Step on one of these at your peril!

Find the odd one out in this stony school.

A stonefish's venom sacs are found in the 13 spines of its dorsal (top) fin.

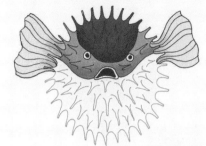

POISONOUS PUFF

Pufferfish can inflate themselves up to several times their regular size to protect them from predators, and they contain a toxin that is deadly to humans and many other fish.

Which silhouette matches this spiny species exactly?

A

B

C

D

E

CHARGED UP

The electric eel possesses special organs that release an electrical charge to stun prey and deter predators.

Z I L A R B

E R U P

Unscramble the letters on each eel to discover three South American countries where this famous freshwater predator can be found.

B I L O C O M A

FINDING FUNGI

Mushrooms are fungi, and unlike plants, they do not need sunlight to make energy for themselves. Truffles are rare mushrooms that grow underground in woodland. Potato-like in appearance, these delicacies are among the world's most expensive foods.

Which hog will sniff out the truffle?

Pigs have been used to hunt for truffles since Roman times, using their exceptional sense of smell.

Mushroom Hunt

R	P	C	H	A	N	T	E	R	E	L	L	E	S
E	I	O	D	N	H	C	Y	G	I	F	Z	J	D
W	B	Y	R	F	V	S	D	T	N	W	D	R	E
O	G	S	U	T	P	E	N	O	K	I	V	Q	A
L	D	T	O	K	O	G	Q	X	C	J	A	S	T
F	Z	E	C	Y	R	B	S	L	A	F	T	O	H
I	W	R	S	Q	T	I	E	R	P	G	X	P	C
L	E	K	G	H	F	R	J	L	Y	V	H	L	A
U	G	V	A	X	O	W	K	R	L	Q	F	U	P
A	J	P	D	M	Z	B	U	T	T	O	N	C	D
C	R	L	T	Y	K	A	E	T	S	F	E	E	B

Many mushroom species are edible, while others are definitely not!

Find these ten types of fungi in the grid. The words may be spelled out in any direction.

BEEFSTEAK
BUTTON
CAULIFLOWER
CHANTERELLE
DEATH CAP
ENOKI
INKCAP
MOREL
OYSTER
PORTOBELLO

Toxic Toadstool

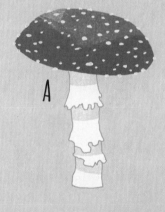

The fly agaric fungus grows in forests and woodlands of Europe, northern Asia, and North America. Look, but don't touch—they are pretty, but poisonous.

Find two toadstools that are exactly the same.

A

D

F

B

C

E

THE AMAZON RAIN FOREST

Located close to the equator, the biggest rain forest in the world provides shelter and food for a vast number of animals. Rain forest trees grow incredibly tall to stretch up to the sunlight.

FINISH

The Amazon rain forest is vast, spanning twice the size of India.

Climb the tree to reach the sunlight at the top.

START

Going Wild

The Amazon rain forest is known to be home to thousands of wild and wonderful species, with new plants and animals being discovered all the time.

Find out what's missing from each sequence below, then draw it in.

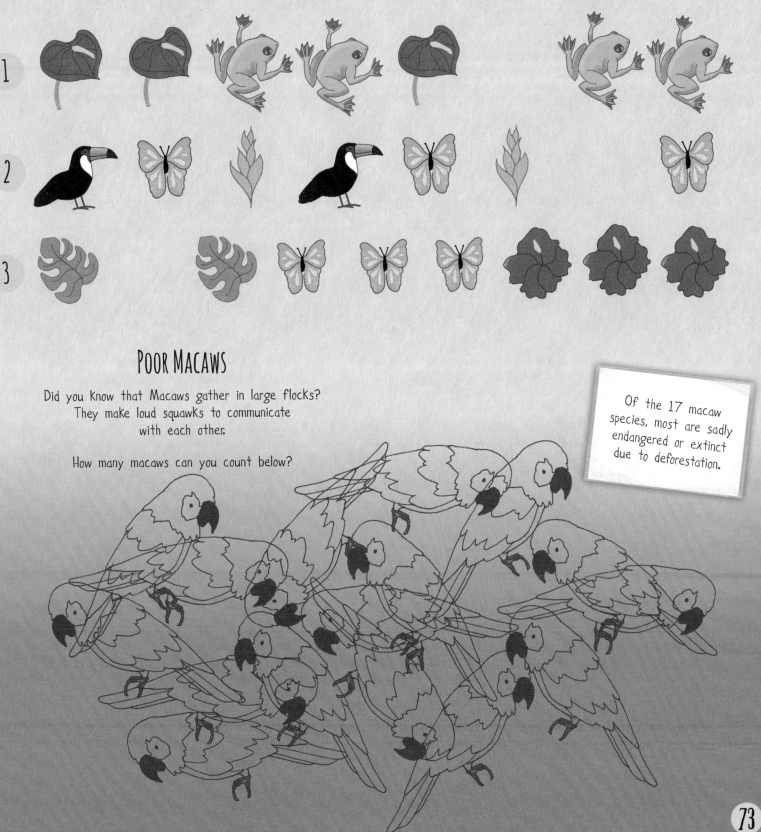

1

2

3

Poor Macaws

Did you know that Macaws gather in large flocks? They make loud squawks to communicate with each other.

How many macaws can you count below?

Of the 17 macaw species, most are sadly endangered or extinct due to deforestation.

THE AMAZON RIVER

The Amazon River, which runs through Brazil, Columbia, Peru, and Venezuela, has the largest volume of fresh water of any river in the world. It's home to some unique wildlife, including the Amazon river dolphin and many fish species.

The Amazon is the world's second-longest river, at over 6,400 km (4,000 mi) long.

Hop across the lily pads, landing on all of the numbers that are multiples of five.

20
5
12
START
25
30
35
11
8
60
40
55
103
10
15
88
7
20
99
34
60
44
100
67
FINISH
85
75

River Reptile

The black caiman is the Amazon River's largest predator. It can grow up to 6 m (almost 20 ft) long. Join the dots to reveal this stealthy hunter.

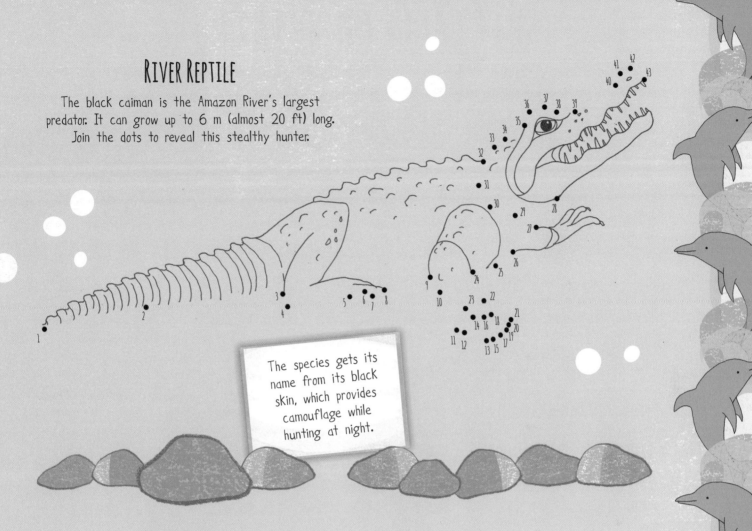

The species gets its name from its black skin, which provides camouflage while hunting at night.

Tooth Fish

Piranhas have lived in the Amazon River for millions of years and are known for their razor-sharp teeth.

Copy the piranha into the empty grid—try drawing one square at a time.

SPECTACULAR SPIDERS

Spiders are arachnids, rather than insects, and can be found on every continent except Antarctica. Most of the 45,000 known species of spiders use a web to catch their prey, which includes anything from small insects to lizards and birds.

Draw lines between the dots to complete this orb-weaver spider's sticky web.

The orb-weaver spider can make the yellow thread of its web brighter or duller by adjusting the amount of pigment in the silk.

Aussie Arachnid

Famous for its red or orange markings, the highly venomous redback spider can be found throughout Australia and parts of Southeast Asia.

Copy the other half of the redback into the grid.

Beat the Eggs!

Female spiders produce either one egg sac with up to about 1,000 eggs inside, or several containing fewer eggs.

Discover the missing numbers in the egg sacs—each number is the total of the two numbers below it.

A
2 3 5

B
12
7
4

C

10
4   7

PLANTS THAT HEAL

For centuries, humans have looked to the plants we grow to provide healing from all sorts of aches, pains, and other medical conditions. Many common garden plants have provided cures in modern medicine.

Can you make your way to the middle of this fragrant lavender maze?

Soothing lavender is said to heal mind and body, and it was used to protect against the plague for centuries— not always successfully!

START

FINISH

Ancient Achillea

One Greek myth tells of Thetis, mother of the ancient Greek hero, Achilles, adding yarrow (also called achillea) when bathing her son. Its protective powers were said to have made Achilles invincible, and the plant was also used to heal soldiers' wounds.

Find these close-up pictures in the yarrow plant.

Healing Harvest

This spiky plant has special qualities— it can heal burns and help digestion.

Unscramble the eight letters hidden on the leaves to find its name.

_ _ _ _   _ _ _ _

MAJESTIC MOUNTAINS

Nine of the ten highest mountains on planet Earth are found in the Himalayas, southern Asia. The tallest of these is the magnificent Mount Everest. Very few people live on the higher slopes of the Himalayan mountains, since the climate is too harsh.

The latest scientific measurements give Mount Everest's elevation to be 8,849 m (29,032 ft) above sea level.

Which climber will reach Everest's snow-capped summit?

1

2

3

4

5

Seeing Red

The endangered red panda is a species threatened by climate change. There are now fewer than 10,000 left in the wild, and most of these are in the Eastern Himalayas.

Copy the red panda's portrait one square at a time.

Beware the Bear!

In the folklore of Nepal, the Yeti is said to be an apelike creature that lives in the Himalayan mountains. In fact, sightings by hikers are more likely to have been of the Himalayan black bear.

Find five differences between the bears in this pair.

GO WITH THE GLOW

Some animals produce a chemical reaction inside their bodies that allows them to light up. This process, called "bioluminescence," is useful as a warning to predators or is sometimes used to attract a mate. Fireflies are famous for their abdomens that glow in the dark.

Circle only the fireflies that show a prime number.

A prime number is a number that can only be divided by itself and 1.

71

37

23

10

11

46

66

6

89

14

3

97

100

53

21

FLASHLIGHT FISH

The lantern fish gets its name from its ability to illuminate the dark, deep waters in which it lives. The light attracts smaller fish to feed on, and it may also be used to charm a mate. Spot the odd one out among this silvery shoal.

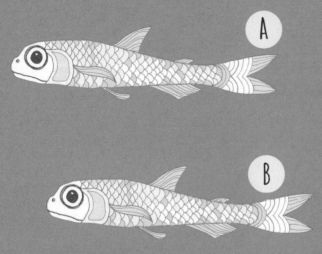

JELLYFISH JUMBLE

The mauve stinger jellyfish leaves a trail of glowing mucus behind if it's startled, while its name in German translates as "night-light." How many shimmering jellyfish make up this bloom?

WATERY WONDERS

When you consider that water covers 71 percent of our planet's surface, it's no surprise that many natural wonders feature water. From spectacular waterfalls to underwater geysers, water amazes above and below sea level.

1 2 3

Angel Falls in Venezuela is the world's highest waterfall on land, dropping an enormous 979 m (3,212 ft).

Choose the path that stretches from the top to the bottom of Angel Falls.

Perfectly Pink

Lake Hillier in Australia is an extraordinary natural wonder, thanks to its bright pink waters! A mix of bacteria and algae present in the salty water give the lake its bubblegum hue.

Which piece does not belong to the lake?

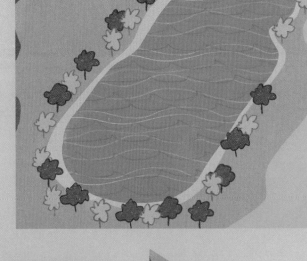

Deep Dive

Deep-sea vents expel water and gas from the ocean floor, causing water temperatures to spike and the nature that lives there to thrive.

Choose the odd number on each geyser to discover when the first deep-sea vent was discovered.

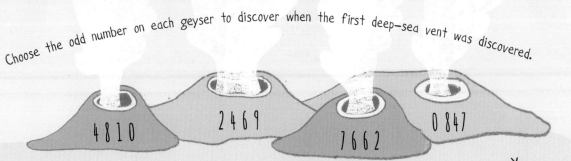

4810   2469   7662   0847

WHAT'S THAT SMELL?

Some animals smell bad for a number of reasons—to warn off predators, mark their territory, or even protect their food. Skunks are regarded as one of the smelliest species on the planet.

Skunks are the size of domestic cats and can be found in the United States, Canada, Latin America, and Mexico.

Rearrange this stinky scene so that the pieces are in the right order.

A   B   C   D   E

UNPLEASANT PHEASANT

The hoatzin, or "stink bird," produces a disgusting, manure-like smell, owing to its leafy diet. Native to the Amazon, this herbivore spends four hours a day chewing huge quantities of foliage.

Fill in this smelly yet elegant fowl.

AN ARTHROPOD'S AROMA

This invertebrate doesn't bite or sting, but certain species do stink! A foul-smelling fluid is released to ward off predators, so handle with care.

D I M P L E L I E

Rearrange the letters above to discover the name of the arthropod.

STRANGE SLEEPERS

Just like humans, animals need sleep to restore their energy levels and
keep themselves healthy. Many species have developed unusual sleeping habits
to protect them from predators or to simply doze for longer.

Sort this sleepy scene puzzle
into the correct order.

Bats are well known for their
habit of sleeping upside down,
which they do to conserve
energy, so that they can
quickly fly away from danger.

1

2

3

4

5

6

POWER NAPPERS

Adult giraffes manage about 30 minutes of sleep
per day, dozing in short five-minute bursts—often
while still standing, and with their eyes open.
Add up the numbers on each giraffe to see
which had the longest amount of sleep.

A ☐   B ☐

2
9
5
7
4
1 8

9 5
1
2
3 6 5

SERIOUS SNOOZERS

When it comes to expert
sleepers, walruses win
flippers down! They can sleep
anywhere—on land,
at the ocean surface, and
even underwater.

Find the odd one out
among this peaceful herd.

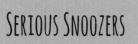

ANSWERS

PAGE 6
Get set, go!

PAGE 7
Swift Swimmer
The black marlin spears fish with its long nose.
All black marlins are born female.

Horsing Around

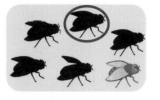

PAGE 8
Tall Trees
A—2,389
B—2,149
C—2,638 (oldest)

PAGE 9
Genuine Giants

Tropical Titan

PAGE 10
Curious Fossils: Ammonite
Amazing Amber: E

PAGE 11
Famous Fossils:
C, E, A, D, B

PAGE 12
In Bloom:
Bird of Paradise

PAGE 13
Titan Arum: 7 times table
Monkeying Around: B and C

PAGE 14
Animals in Danger: the Adult
Mango Mix-up: Orangutan

PAGE 15
Feeling Blue: 16 whales

PAGE 16
The Great Barrier Reef: 5,2,1,6,4,3

PAGE 17
Pretty Parrotfish

Underwater Treasures

PAGE 18
Brilliant Beetles: C. 127−26=101

PAGE 19
Horned Herbivores

Musical Bug: Violin Beetle

PAGE 20
Changing Seasons:
Yes, 44 Cherries

PAGE 21
Beautiful Blossoms

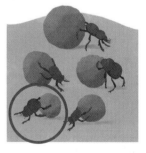

Falling Leaves

PAGE 22
Desert Conditions

PAGE 23
Desert Storm

Too Cold to Snow: e,c,b,a,d

PAGE 24 Desert Dwellers

B

PAGE 25
Super Survivors:
shadow c

Saharan Snakes:
Egyptian Cobra

PAGE 26
Cool Crystals

PAGE 27
Unearthing Geodes: C

PAGE 28
Jaw-Dropping Jumpers

PAGE 29
Legendary Leapers

Jump on Board!: B does not belong.

PAGE 30
All About Algae

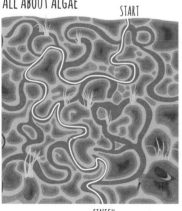

START

FINISH

PAGE 31
Incredible Algae

Giant Grower

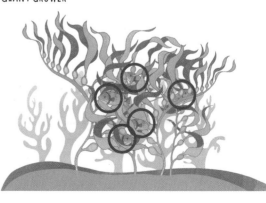

R	T	G	H	L	B	Y	D	W	J	I	F	Q	C
X	S	U	A	N	I	M	A	L	F	E	E	D	I
S	U	R	F	B	O	A	R	D	S	B	R	H	T
H	D	C	V	S	F	W	Y	K	U	X	T	L	S
B	O	B	X	Q	U	J	O	S	L	H	I	J	A
I	J	I	F	M	E	V	C	F	K	W	L	V	L
G	K	H	L	O	L	E	Y	B	S	M	I	G	P
V	F	M	W	K	O	H	J	E	C	O	Z	K	O
Y	Q	P	S	M	E	D	I	C	I	N	E	S	I
S	E	O	H	S	G	N	I	N	N	U	R	L	B

91

PAGE 32
Wings of Wonder

PAGE 33
Wandering Wonder:

A	B	C	D	E	F	G	H	I	J	K	K	M
Z	Y	X	W	V	U	T	S	R	Q	P	O	N

N	O	P	Q	R	S	T	U	V	W	X	Y	Z
M	L	K	J	I	H	G	F	E	D	C	B	A

ALBATROSS

Flightless Functions:
- ☑ mating displays
- ☑ fans to keep cool
- ☑ to balance when running
- ☑ for defending themselves
- ☐ camouflage

PAGE 34
The Water Cycle

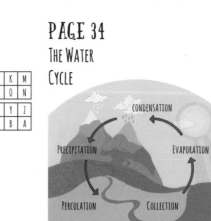

CONDENSATION

Precipitation

Evaporation

Percolation

Collection

PAGE 35
Shifting States

LIQUID   SOLID   GAS

Fast Floods

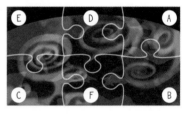

PAGE 36
Fact or Fairy tale?

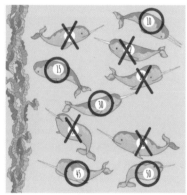

PAGE 37
Amazing Amphibian

PAGE 38
Tropical Storms

PAGE 39
Swirling Storm

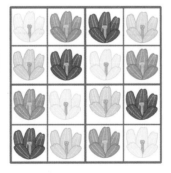

PAGE 40
Natural Treasures

PAGE 41
Saffron Sudoku

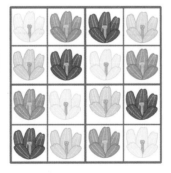

LUXURY FABRIC: GOAT B

PAGE 42
Precious Metals

PAGE 43
Gold Rush

1383

432 951

199 233 718

149 50 183 535

PAGE 44
All About Clouds

START

FINISH

PAGE 45
Changing Clouds

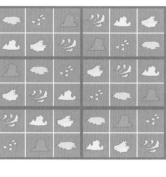

Precipitation Puzzle

A — Rain—Falling drops of liquid water

B — Sleet—Rain that freezes as it falls

C — Hail—Falling balls of ice

D — Snow—Falling ice crystals

PAGE 46
Prickly Plants: Succulent

PAGE 47
Spiky Saguaro   Ant Allies

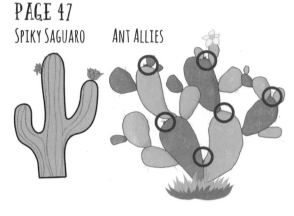

PAGE 48
Wonderful Butterflies

4

2

5

6

1

3

PAGE 49
Butterflies of Europe

PAGE 50
Rugged Rocks

 A4

A2

C4

PAGE 51
Sacred Site

A

B

Giant's Causeway

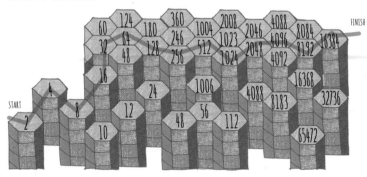

FINISH

60 124 180 360 1004 2008 2046 4088 8084 16384

32 64 128 246 512 1023 4096 8192

48 256 1024 2048 4092

16 24 1006 4088 16368 32736

8 12 56 8183

4 48 112 16368

2 10 65472

START

93

PAGE 52 Arctic Adaptions

PAGE 53 Polar Pal

Frequent Flyer: 17 Arctic Terns

PAGE 55 Trapped!

Bogus Bug-eater

| 1 | 5 | 2 |

PAGE 56 Amazing Bees Start

Finish

PAGE 57

Ingenious
Insects

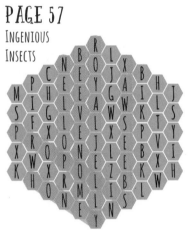

Cutting Edge: Branch B

PAGE 58 Nature's Rainbow

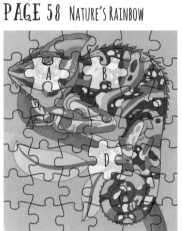

PAGE 59 In the Pink

PAGE 60

Explosive
volcanoes

PAGE 61

Deep-sea Danger: Submarine
Eruption Disruption: 16 letters

PAGE 62

Glistening Gemstones

PAGE 63

Ancient Treasures   Hidden Gems

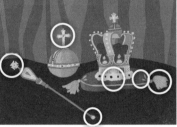

PAGE 64

Incredible
Journeys:
45 Crabs

PAGE 65
Turtle Tourists: green, leatherback, loggerhead

Migrant Monarch:

Start
Finish

PAGE 66 The Northern Lights

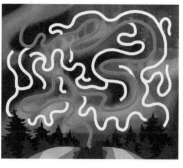

PAGE 67 Alaskan Aurora

A
B
C
D

PAGE 68 Deadly Predators

1
2
3
4

PAGE 69
Poisonous Puff

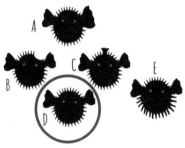
A
B
C
D
E

Charged Up
Brazil, Peru, Colombia

PAGE 70
Finding Fungi

PAGE 71
Mushroom Hunt

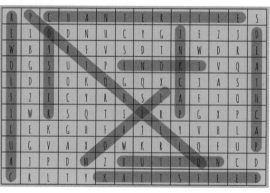

Toxic Toadstool:
A and F

PAGE 72
The Amazon Rain forest

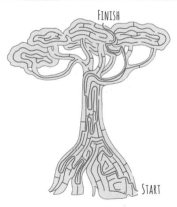
Finish
Start

PAGE 73
Going Wild

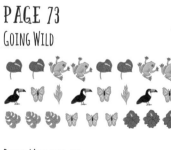

Poor Macaws: 16 macaws

PAGE 74
The Amazon River

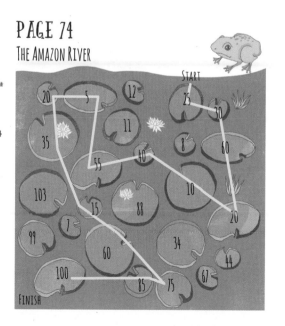

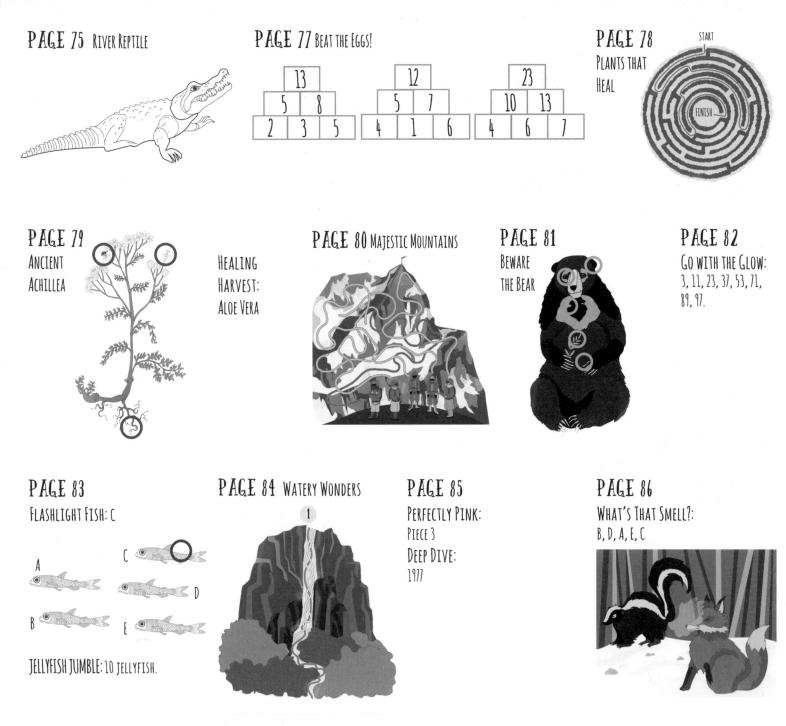

PAGE 75 River Reptile

PAGE 77 Beat the Eggs!

	13			12			23	
5		8	5		7		10	13
2	3	5	4	1	6	4	6	7

PAGE 78 Plants that Heal

START
FINISH

PAGE 79 Ancient Achillea

Healing Harvest: Aloe Vera

PAGE 80 Majestic Mountains

PAGE 81 Beware the Bear

PAGE 82 Go with the Glow: 3, 11, 23, 37, 53, 71, 89, 97.

PAGE 83

Flashlight Fish: C

A
C
B
D
E

Jellyfish Jumble: 10 jellyfish.

PAGE 84 Watery Wonders

1

PAGE 85

Perfectly Pink: Piece 3

Deep Dive: 1977

PAGE 86

What's That Smell?: B, D, A, E, C

PAGE 87

An Arthropod's Aroma: millipede.

PAGE 88 Strange Sleepers

2 1 5
6 4 3

PAGE 89

Power Nappers:
Giraffe A: 36 minutes
Giraffe B: 31 minutes

Serious Snoozers: